The Adventures Of
SUPERCAPTAINBRAVEMAN

Book 1:
A Day at the Park

by Jennifer & Paul Norman
Pictures by Victor Lodevico
Introduction by Sharon Buchalter

BALDHEAD MAN PRODUCTIONS, INC.

Copyright © 2016 by Baldhead Man Productions, Inc.

All rights reserved.
No part of this publication may be reproduced or transmitted in any form or by any means, electronic or mechanical, including photocopying, recording, or any information storage and retrieval system, without permission in writing from the publisher.

Requests for permission to reproduce any part of this book should be directed to info@supercaptainbraveman.com.

Summary: A young, disabled boy dreams and turns into his alter ego, SuperCaptainBraveMan, to help a handicapped girl make new friends.

SUPERCAPTAINBRAVEMAN is a trademark of Baldhead Man Productions, Inc.

www.supercaptainbraveman.com

Book design © 2016, Baldhead Man Productions, Inc.
Text by Jennifer and Paul Norman
Illustrations by Victor Lodevico

First Edition

Printed in China

ISBN 978-0-9973162-0-9

This book is dedicated to and inspired by our beloved son Kyle,
who is living proof that love, hope and persistence
create miracles every day.

A Note to Parents and Educators

Kids are a delight, and they are fascinated by the world.

One particular boy named Kyle finds joy in bringing different people together.

Like all young boys and girls, Kyle has hopes and dreams despite having challenges. Kyle's primary challenge is a rare disorder that impacts his health and mobility. Special equipment and hands-on nursing care are part of Kyle's everyday life.

Recognizing the discomfort often felt in the presence of differently-abled individuals, the SuperCaptainBraveMan series strives to educate youth on values of compassion, inclusion and friendship.

The main character is based on a student that I home school. The series is written by Kyle's parents, Jennifer and Paul. The pictures are drawn by Kyle's nurse and buddy for life, Victor.

As you read and share this home-grown series, may your heart be lifted, and may your children find inspiration to cherish each other's differences.

Sharon Buchalter
Special Education Teacher

Meet Kyle

Kyle is a young boy with a big heart. He is smart, curious, and always very happy. Kyle lives at home with his mommy, daddy, older sister and little dog Mochi.

Kyle has extra special things to help him each day, because his body doesn't make as much energy as other kids his age.

First, Kyle has a wheelchair. It helps him move around.

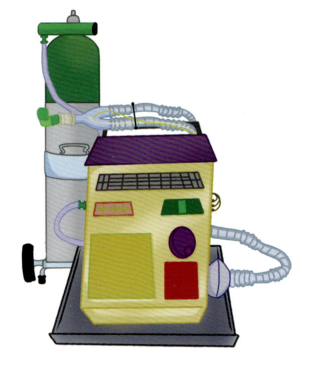

Next, Kyle has a little machine called a ventilator. It helps him breathe better.

And last, Kyle has a little spout on his tummy called a g-tube button. It's like one you blow into on a beach ball. Liquid formula gets piped through the g-tube button into Kyle's tummy when it's time for him to eat.

When Kyle wakes up, nurse Brigette gets him ready to start a new day. They meet mommy, daddy and sister in the kitchen for breakfast.

Nurse Brigette prepares Kyle's formula. She has an idea.

"Would you like to go to the park today, Kyle?" she asks.

"Yes please!" answers Kyle, "Can Mochi come, too?"

"Of course!" replies nurse Brigette.

"Woof!" barks Mochi happily.

After breakfast, nurse Brigette helps Kyle into his wheelchair.

She buckles his seatbelt, then steers toward the park.

Mochi follows along, not wanting to miss out on the fun!

When they reach the park, nurse Brigette surprises Kyle with bubbles!

Kyle lifts his wand and watches as the bubbles float through the park.

Kyle notices a class of students playing nearby. He is happy to see the kids having so much fun.

The children notice the bubbles and notice Kyle, too, but they are too shy to say hi.

At the end of the day, mommy and daddy tuck Kyle into bed.

Mommy reads a story, then daddy hands Kyle his favorite sleepy toys.

"Time for sleep," mommy and daddy whisper with kisses good night.

Nurse Brigette dims the light as Kyle closes his eyes.

Kyle thinks about his fun day as he falls into a very deep sleep.

Not before long, he starts to dream...

Kyle dreams that he does not need a special wheelchair for moving, or a ventilator for breathing, or a g-tube for eating.

Kyle dreams instead that he has special powers inside him.

He dreams he turns into...

SUPERCAPTAINBRAVEMAN!!!

SuperCaptainBraveMan is so courageous, he can do anything!

He never tires and is never afraid.

He comes to kids' rescue when they are feeling sad, unwell or scared.

With SuperCaptainBraveMan as your friend, you'll discover your own power to become a hero, too!

SuperCaptainBraveMan soars to his favorite park.

He sees kids playing down below.

"Look! It's SuperCaptainBraveMan!" Frankie points and hollers.

"Hooray! He's coming to see us!" Gene waves and shouts.

The kids are so excited, they greet SuperCaptainBraveMan with cheers and smiles.

"Would you like to play a game with us?" asks Gene.

"Sure!" replies SuperCaptainBraveMan.

But just then, he notices a girl in the distance.

She is in a wheelchair.

She is all alone and looks sad.

"Hmmm," thinks SuperCaptainBraveMan, "It's not right for her to feel left out. I know I don't like feeling that way. Maybe there's something I can do to help."

With that, he walks over to say hi.

"Hi, I'm SuperCaptainBraveMan. What's your name?" he asks.

"I'm Emily," she replies.

"I really like your wheelchair. Is it new?"

"Uh-huh. I had an accident, and now my legs don't work very well."

"I understand. Say, the kids and I are about to play a game. Please join us!"

"Me? Oh, no, I can't. Maybe I'll just watch."

"Don't worry, when you're with me, you don't have to be afraid."

"Well, ok," Emily decides to trust SuperCaptainBraveMan and be brave.

"Hey everyone," SuperCaptainBraveMan calls out. "Meet Emily. She's going to play with us."

"Huh?" Frankie mumbles. "That girl is in a wheelchair. How is she going to play with us? She can't run like we can."

"Maybe not," says Gene, "but I'm sure there's a fun game we can all play."

Gene introduces himself to Emily with a smile. Emily feels happy to make a new friend.

SuperCaptainBraveMan has an idea. "Let's play tag! Emily and I can be it! On the count of three, you better start running!"

One... Two...

THREE!!!

In a flash, the kids race down the path in a frenzy, trying not to get tagged.

SuperCaptainBraveMan makes sure Emily is buckled in, then they both take off like a rocket.

Faster and faster they zoom down the path!

Emily can't contain her joy. She feels like she's flying!

She can't believe she is gaining on the other kids!

Just a few feet further! She reaches out her arm and...

"Frankie is it!" Emily shouts as she grasps Frankie's arm.

Frankie laughs as he slows down to catch his breath.

"Way to go, Emily!" Frankie cheers. "I'm really glad you came to play tag with us."

"Me too!" says Emily, "I was nervous at first, but then I decided to be brave and join in. It was a lot of fun!"

"Hooray, Emily! Hooray, SuperCaptainBraveMan!" all the kids exclaim.

"Thank you my friend!" Emily gives SuperCaptainBraveMan a big hug.

"Now I'm not afraid to play with other kids. It's okay that I'm in a wheelchair. There are still lots of things we can do together that are fun."

"That's right, Emily," SuperCaptainBraveMan assures. "You can do amazing things when you decide to try."

So with that, SuperCaptainBraveMan says goodbye to each of his new friends and dashes off with a puff into the sky.

As he heads back home, the slightest sound catches his ear...

Nurse Brigette turns off Kyle's bedroom light.

Kyle pretends to still be asleep as nurse Brigette places a fresh sleepy toy by his side.

"Good night, Kyle," whispers Brigette as she tiptoes out the door for the night.

"You mean, 'Good night, SuperCaptainBraveMan,'" winks Kyle.

THE END.

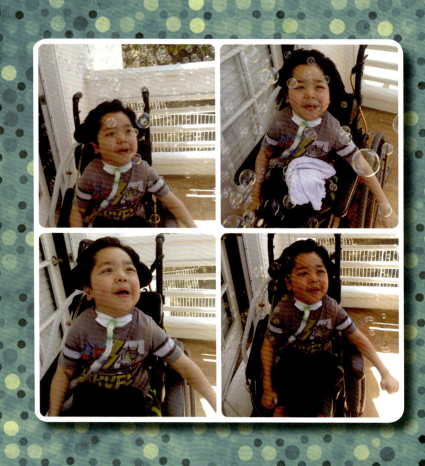

ACKNOWLEDGEMENTS

Special thanks go out to our family and friends for all the love and support they give us each and every day.

Big bear hugs go out to all Kyle's amazing nurses and caretakers, present and past, especially Victor Lodevico, Sally del Rosario-Bada, Brigette Vasquez, Nancy Ruiz, Leah Lodevico, Samantha Shippee, Ashley Butterfield, Eva Becerra, Sanci Toledo, Manfred Rantner, Nicholas Russell, Kim Lindstadt and Emy Chai.

High fives go to Kyle's rockstar doctors and researchers, especially Dr. Richard Kelley, Dr. Peter Waldstein, Dr. Julia White, Dr. Danica Schulte, Dr. Pedro Sanchez, Dr. Christopher Harris, Dr. Robert Kay, Dr. Ryan Kotton, Dr. Harry Cynamon, Dr. Elaine Kamil, Dr. Gene Liu, Dr. Arthur Wu, Dr. Robert Smith, Dr. Lilian Sababa, Dr. Philip Frykman and Dr. Tyler Pierson.

Major points go to Kyle's present and past physical therapists, Larry Sulham and Jill (Masutomi) Ordorica.

A gold star goes to Kyle's teacher, Sharon Buchalter.

Fist bumps go to Kyle's respiratory therapists, Ivan Puno and Randy Soriano.

A shout out goes to the United Mitochondrial Disease Foundation (UMDF).

ABOUT THE NORMANS

Paul and Jennifer Norman are native New Yorkers who met while working in Los Angeles. In 2006, they were thrilled to welcome their son Kyle to the world.

In 2008, at the age of two, Kyle began showing signs of erratic movement and increasing weakness – what doctors call ataxia. Kyle's symptoms worsened until ultimately he drifted into a comatose state. After months in the PICU, Kyle was diagnosed with a rare mitochondrial disorder. Though the prognosis for his condition was bleak, somehow Kyle managed to beat the odds and show signs of recovery.

At the time of this printing, Kyle is nine years old. Though limited in his physical abilities, those who know Kyle are amazed by his extraordinary inner strength and the light that emanates from his soul. Truly, Kyle has managed to share countless life lessons with his family, friends and fans all over the world, just by being himself.

The SuperCaptainBraveMan series is authored to pay homage to those valuable life lessons, celebrating people of all backgrounds and all abilities with kindness, compassion and friendship.

Co-authors Paul and Jennifer Norman with their son Kyle, Los Angeles, 2009.